MW00914952

soaring to new heights

A Kid's Guide to Becoming a Pilot

sarah michaels

contents

introduction

up, up, and away!

Once upon a time, in a small town called Windsville, there was a curious 10-year-old named Alex. Alex was fascinated by airplanes and often daydreamed about flying high above the clouds. They loved to read books about pilots, aircraft, and the science of flight. Alex's room was filled with airplane models and posters of various aircraft. They had always dreamt of taking to the skies, but they had never actually been on an airplane.

One day, Alex's parents surprised them with the most exciting news: they were going on a family vacation to a faraway island, and they would all be flying there! Alex's eyes sparkled with excitement as they imagined soaring through the air and looking down at the world from above.

The days leading up to the flight felt like an eternity to Alex. They spent their time packing and repacking their bags, making sure they had all their favorite airplane books and toys for the journey. They couldn't stop talking about the upcoming adventure, sharing their excitement with friends at school and family members.

Finally, the big day arrived. Alex woke up extra early, eager to head to the airport. The family loaded up their luggage and set off for the adventure of a lifetime. As they approached the airport, Alex's heart raced with anticipation. They could hardly believe that in just a few hours, they would be up in the sky, experiencing the thrill of flight for the first time.

The airport was bustling with activity. People from all walks of life were coming and going, and Alex couldn't help but wonder about their stories. Where were they traveling? What kind of adventures awaited them? Alex's eyes widened as they spotted the pilots and flight attendants in their uniforms, striding confidently through the airport. It was like seeing their heroes in person, and Alex's admiration for these skilled professionals grew even more.

As Alex and their family made their way through the airport, they marveled at the massive planes outside the terminal windows. There were all sorts of aircraft, from small private planes to enormous commercial airliners. Alex could hardly contain their excitement as they tried to identify each type of plane.

Soon enough, it was time to board. Alex clutched their ticket tightly, taking a deep breath as they stepped onto the jet bridge. Their heart pounded with anticipation, knowing that the moment they had been waiting for was just a few steps away.

The inside of the airplane was even more impressive than Alex had imagined. Rows and rows of seats stretched down the aisle, with the cockpit door at the front, where the pilots were busy preparing for takeoff. Alex couldn't help but sneak a peek through the tiny window in the cockpit door, catching a glimpse of the pilots at work. It was like witnessing magic in action.

As they found their seats, Alex immediately buckled up and looked out the window, eager to see the plane's massive wings and engines. The flight attendants bustled around the cabin, ensuring everyone was settled in and ready for takeoff. Alex listened intently to the safety instructions, determined to learn everything they could about the flight experience.

The moment had finally arrived. The engines roared to life, and the plane started to move. Alex's eyes were glued to the window as they watched the ground crews waving goodbye, and the airport buildings slowly began to shrink. The plane gathered speed, and Alex could feel the force pressing them back into their seat.

Suddenly, the wheels left the ground, and they were airborne! Alex gasped in wonder as the plane soared higher and higher into the sky. The houses and cars below became tiny specks, and the world seemed to stretch out endlessly in all directions. It was an incredible feeling, like being on top of the world.

Alex's excitement only grew as they gazed out the window during the flight. They marveled at the cotton-candy clouds and the vast, blue sky that seemed to go on forever. It was a magical world up here, and Alex felt like they were a part of something truly special.

During the flight, Alex took the opportunity to ask a friendly flight attendant some questions about airplanes and the life of a pilot. The flight attendant happily obliged, sharing fascinating facts and stories about the world of aviation. Alex listened intently, soaking up every word, and feeling more inspired than ever to pursue their dream of becoming a pilot.

All too soon, the plane began its descent. The island destination came into view, with its beautiful beaches and sparkling blue waters. As the plane touched down, Alex felt a mix of emotions. They were sad that the flight was over but thrilled about the adventure they had just experienced.

As the family disembarked, Alex looked back at the plane, grateful for the journey it had taken them on. They knew that this first flight had ignited a passion inside them, a passion they would carry with them for the rest of their lives. As they left the airport and set off for their island vacation, Alex made a promise to themselves: one day, they would be the one in the cockpit, taking passengers on their own magical journeys through the skies.

And so, with their heart full of dreams and determination, Alex began their journey toward becoming a pilot. From that day on, they knew that the sky was not the limit – it was just the beginning.

what's inside this adventure

Now that you've joined Alex on their incredible first flight, I'm sure you're as excited as they were to learn all about becoming a pilot. In this book, we'll take you on a journey through the world of aviation, exploring different aspects of flying and the steps you'll need to take to become a pilot.

Our adventure begins with a trip back in time to discover the history of aviation. We'll learn about the brave pioneers who took to the skies and changed the world forever. You'll meet famous pilots like the Wright Brothers, Amelia Earhart, and Charles Lindbergh, and find out about the amazing aircraft they flew. This section will help you understand how aviation has evolved over the years and the incredible progress that has been made.

Next, we'll dive into the different types of aircraft you might encounter on your journey to becoming a pilot. From small single-engine planes to gigantic commercial airliners, each type of aircraft has its own unique characteristics and uses. You'll learn about the various parts of an airplane and how they work together to make flight possible.

Once you're familiar with the basics of aviation, we'll take a closer look at the path to becoming a pilot. You'll discover the essential requirements you'll need to meet, like age and education, as well as vision and health standards. We'll also explore the different types of pilot licenses, from student pilot to commercial pilot, and the steps you'll need to take to earn each one.

Now that you know what it takes to become a pilot, we'll guide you through the training and education process. We'll start with ground school, where you'll learn the fundamentals of aerodynamics, aircraft systems, navigation, and flight planning. Then, we'll move on to flight school, where you'll experience hands-on training in preflight preparation, basic flight maneuvers, takeoffs and landings, and cross-country flights. Finally, we'll discuss how to pass the FAA written and practical exams that are required to earn your pilot's license.

Of course, becoming a pilot opens up a whole world of exciting career possibilities. In the following sections, we'll explore some of the many aviation careers you might consider. You'll learn about the lives of commercial airline pilots, corporate or charter pilots, military pilots, and flight instructors. We'll also introduce you to other aviation-related careers, such as air traffic controllers and aircraft mechanics, so you can see the full spectrum of opportunities available in this amazing field.

But what's it really like to be a pilot? In our next section, we'll give you a glimpse into the daily routine of a pilot, discussing the importance of safety and professionalism in the job. You'll also learn about the challenges and rewards of a career in aviation, giving you a better understanding of what to expect as you embark on this exciting journey.

As you work toward your dream of becoming a pilot, you'll want to take advantage of every opportunity to learn and grow. In our tips for aspiring pilots section, we'll share some great ways to immerse yourself in the world of aviation. You'll learn about joining aviation clubs or organizations, attending air shows and visiting aviation museums, reading books and magazines on the subject, networking with pilots and aviation professionals, and participating in aviation camps and workshops.

Finally, we'll wrap up our adventure with some words of encouragement and inspiration. We'll remind you that the sky is not the limit; it's just the beginning of your journey. No matter where your dreams take you, remember that hard work, dedication, and a love for flying can help you soar to new heights.

Are you ready to embark on this incredible adventure and learn all about the world of aviation? Just like Alex, you too can take to the skies and make your dreams come true. With each page, you'll gain the knowledge and inspiration you need to pursue a career as a pilot or simply develop a deeper appreciation for the magic of flight.

As you read through this book, we hope you'll feel the same sense of wonder and excitement that Alex experienced during their first flight. We encourage you to ask questions, seek out new information, and share your love for aviation with others. Who knows? You might even inspire someone else to pursue their own dreams of flying!

So, strap in, and get ready for takeoff. This adventure is about to begin, and the skies are waiting for you to explore them. With every section, you'll be one step closer to achieving your dream of becoming a pilot or simply enjoying the incredible world of aviation.

As we embark on this journey together, always remember that the sky's the limit. Keep your dreams alive and your passion for flight burning bright, and one day, you might just find yourself soaring through the clouds, just like Alex.

chasing your dreams, one flight at a time

You've now joined Alex on their first flight and explored the contents of this book. It's the perfect time to talk about something very important: the significance of pursuing your dreams. Dreams are the fuel that keeps us moving forward, helping us to aim high and achieve great things. In this section, we'll discuss why it's crucial to chase your dreams, no matter how big or small they may be.

Dreams give us purpose and direction. When you have a dream, you have a goal to work towards. For Alex, their dream was to become a pilot, and this goal motivated them to learn more about aviation and work hard to make that dream a reality. When you have a clear dream in mind, you're more likely to stay focused and put in the effort needed to achieve your goals.

Chasing your dreams also helps build confidence

and self-esteem. When you believe in yourself and your ability to achieve your dreams, you'll develop a strong sense of self-worth. Each small step you take towards your goal will make you feel more capable and confident. As you gain new skills and knowledge, you'll grow as a person and learn to trust in your own abilities.

Pursuing your dreams can also lead to personal growth and development. When you work towards a goal, you often encounter challenges and obstacles that require you to learn and adapt. Facing these challenges helps you develop resilience, problem-solving skills, and determination. Overcoming obstacles not only brings you closer to your dream but also helps you become a stronger, more resourceful person.

Another reason to chase your dreams is that it can inspire others. When people see you working hard to achieve your goals, they may feel motivated to pursue their own dreams. Alex's passion for aviation and determination to become a pilot might inspire others to explore the world of flight or to follow their own unique dreams. By sharing your journey and your successes, you can become a positive role model for friends, family, and even strangers who learn about your story.

Working towards your dreams can also lead to a more fulfilling life. When you're passionate about something and put in the time and effort to achieve your goals, you'll experience a sense of accomplishment and satisfaction that's hard to beat. Even if the road to your dream is challenging, the rewards you'll reap along the way will make the journey worth it.

Now, you might be wondering how to start pursuing your dreams, especially if they seem big or far away. Here are a few tips to help you get started:

1. Set clear and achievable goals: Break your dream down into smaller, manageable steps. This will help you stay focused and make progress without feeling overwhelmed. For example, if your dream is to become a pilot, start by researching the requirements and steps you need to take, such as attending ground school and flight training.

2. Be persistent: Chasing your dreams takes time and effort. There will be setbacks and obstacles along the way, but it's important to keep pushing forward. Stay dedicated to your goals and remind yourself why your dream is important to you.

3. Learn from your mistakes: Nobody's perfect, and we all make mistakes. When you stumble or face challenges, use these experiences as opportunities to grow and learn. This will help you become more resilient and better equipped to tackle future obstacles.

4. Surround yourself with support: Pursuing your dreams can be a lot easier when you have a strong

support network. Share your goals with friends and family, and seek out mentors or role models who can offer guidance and encouragement. Join clubs or organizations related to your dream, where you can connect with others who share your passion.

5. Celebrate your achievements: As you make progress towards your dream, don't forget to acknowledge and celebrate your successes, big and small. This will help keep you motivated and remind you of how far you've come.

Throughout this book, as we explore the world of aviation and the path to becoming a pilot, remember that your dreams are worth chasing. Just like Alex, you have the power to turn your dreams into reality by working hard, staying focused, and believing in yourself.

As you continue on this journey, always remember that the sky is not the limit—it's just the beginning. Whether your dream is to become a pilot, an astronaut, a doctor, or anything else, the most important thing is to believe in yourself and never give up.

Let this book be your guide as you learn more about the exciting world of aviation, and may it inspire you to chase your dreams and reach for the stars. Your adventure is just beginning, and there's no telling how high you'll soar when you follow your heart and believe in your dreams.

1 /
discovering aviation

sky pioneers - a glimpse into aviation history

ARE you ready to embark on a thrilling journey through time? In this section, we'll explore the fascinating history of aviation and meet some of the incredible pilots who dared to reach for the skies. Strap in and join us as we travel back to the early days of flight and learn about the brave pioneers who changed the world forever.

Our story begins in the late 18th century with the invention of the hot air balloon. Two French brothers, Joseph-Michel and Jacques-Étienne Montgolfier, designed the first hot air balloon in 1783. These balloons, filled with hot air, became the first successful human-carrying flight technology. While they couldn't be steered or controlled, they laid the foundation for future developments in aviation.

Fast forward to the late 19th century, when inventors began experimenting with gliders—aircraft that could glide through the air without an engine. Otto Lilienthal, a German aviation pioneer, was one of the first people to design, build, and fly gliders successfully. His groundbreaking work laid the groundwork for the future of powered flight.

Now, let's meet two of the most famous pilots in history: the Wright Brothers. Orville and Wilbur Wright, two American brothers, were the first to invent a successful airplane powered by an engine. In 1903, they made history when their aircraft, the Wright Flyer, took to the skies for the first time in Kitty Hawk, North Carolina. Their incredible achievements paved the way for modern aviation as we know it.

As airplanes continued to evolve, so did the pilots who flew them. One such pilot was Charles Lindbergh, who made history in 1927 by completing the first solo nonstop flight across the Atlantic Ocean. He flew from New York to Paris in a single-engine aircraft called the Spirit of St. Louis, proving that long-distance air travel was possible.

Another trailblazing pilot you might have heard of

is Amelia Earhart. She was the first woman to fly solo across the Atlantic Ocean in 1932. Earhart was also the first person to fly solo from Hawaii to California, and she set numerous speed and distance records during her career. Despite her mysterious disappearance during an attempt to circumnavigate the globe in 1937, Earhart remains an inspiration for pilots and dreamers everywhere.

As aviation technology progressed, so too did the daring feats of pilots. In 1947, American pilot Chuck Yeager achieved the unthinkable by becoming the first person to fly faster than the speed of sound. He accomplished this incredible feat in the Bell X-1, a rocket-powered aircraft specially designed to test the limits of high-speed flight.

Throughout the 20th century, military pilots also played a significant role in advancing aviation. During World War I and II, pilots in fighter and bomber aircraft were instrumental in shaping the outcomes of these conflicts. Military pilots have continued to push the boundaries of flight technology, leading to the development of advanced jet aircraft and even stealth technology.

The world of aviation isn't just limited to airplanes, though. The Space Race between the United States and the Soviet Union in the mid-20th century opened up a whole new frontier for pilots. Soviet cosmonaut Yuri Gagarin became the first human to journey into outer space in 1961, while American astronaut Neil Armstrong became the first person to set foot on the moon in 1969.

Today, pilots continue to make history and push the boundaries of flight. From commercial airline pilots to test pilots working on cutting-edge aircraft, these brave men and women are carrying on the legacy of the pioneers who came before them.

As you can see, the history of aviation is filled with incredible stories of courage , determination, and innovation. These pioneering pilots not only changed the way we travel, but they also expanded our understanding of what is possible when we dare to dream big.

Now that you've learned about some of the amazing people who helped shape the world of aviation, you might be feeling even more inspired to chase your own dreams of flight. As you continue on your journey to become a pilot, remember that you're following in the footsteps of these courageous trailblazers who defied the odds and conquered the skies.

The history of aviation shows us that anything is possible when we believe in ourselves and work hard to achieve our goals. Whether you dream of flying commercial airliners, piloting spacecraft, or simply exploring the skies for the sheer joy of it, remember that you too can become part of this incredible story.

As we move forward through this book and dive deeper into the world of aviation, keep the lessons of these pioneering pilots in mind. Their determination, ingenuity, and passion for flight can serve as a guiding light as you navigate your own path towards becoming a pilot.

So, take a moment to dream big and imagine yourself soaring through the skies, just like the Wright Brothers, Amelia Earhart, and all the other remarkable pilots who have come before you. Who knows? Maybe one day, you'll make history and inspire others to reach for the stars as well.

Now that we've explored the past, it's time to learn about the present and look towards the future of aviation. In the coming sections, we'll delve into the different types of aircraft, the steps you need to take to become a pilot, and the exciting careers that await you in the world of aviation. Are you ready to spread your wings and fly? The adventure is just beginning, and the sky is waiting for you to explore it.

a sky full of possibilities - exploring different types of aircraft

In this section, we'll introduce you to various types of aircraft and their uses, from small gliders to massive airliners and everything in between. Ready to discover the fascinating world of flying machines? Let's get started!

1. Gliders: We've already mentioned gliders when we talked about Otto Lilienthal, but let's take a closer look at these unique aircraft. Gliders, also known as sailplanes, are lightweight aircraft that don't have engines. Instead, they use the natural lift created by air currents to stay aloft. Gliders are used for recreational flying, teaching the basics of flight, and even for competitive gliding events.

2. Single-engine propeller planes: These are the most common type of small aircraft you'll see at your local airport. They have a single piston engine and a propeller at the front. Single-engine planes are used for various purposes, including flight training, recreational flying, and short-distance transportation. Some well-known examples include the Cessna 172 and the Piper Cherokee.

3. Multi-engine propeller planes: These aircraft have two or more piston engines, which provide more power and reliability than single-engine planes. Multi-

engine propeller planes are often used for transporting small groups of passengers, cargo, or for specialized tasks like aerial mapping and firefighting. Examples include the Beechcraft Baron and the Piper Navajo.

4. Helicopters: Unlike airplanes, helicopters have rotating blades called rotors that allow them to take off and land vertically. This unique ability makes helicopters perfect for a wide range of jobs, such as search and rescue, medical transportation, and even aerial tours. Some well-known helicopters include the Bell 206 JetRanger and the Sikorsky UH-60 Black Hawk.

5. Jets: These speedy aircraft use jet engines instead of propellers for propulsion. Jets are typically faster and can fly higher than propeller-driven planes, making them ideal for long-distance travel. There are many different types of jets, ranging from small private jets like the Cessna Citation to massive commercial airliners like the Boeing 747 and the Airbus A380.

6. Military aircraft: The military uses various types of aircraft for different purposes, such as fighter jets for air-to-air combat, bombers for attacking ground targets, and cargo planes for transporting troops and supplies. Some famous military aircraft include the F-16 Fighting Falcon, the B-2 Spirit stealth bomber, and the massive C-130 Hercules transport plane.

7. Seaplanes and amphibious aircraft: These unique aircraft are designed to take off and land on water,

making them perfect for operations in remote areas or for island-hopping adventures. Seaplanes have floats instead of wheels, while amphibious aircraft can switch between land and water operations. Examples of these versatile aircraft include the de Havilland Beaver and the Grumman Goose.

8. Drones and unmanned aerial vehicles (UAVs): Drones are remotely piloted or autonomous aircraft that come in various shapes and sizes. They're used for a wide range of applications, from aerial photography and surveying to military reconnaissance and even package delivery. Some popular drones include the DJI Phantom and the military's MQ-9 Reaper.

As you can see, the world of aviation is full of diverse and fascinating aircraft, each with its unique abilities and uses. No matter what type of flying sparks your interest, there's an aircraft out there waiting for you to explore and master.

As you continue your journey through this book, keep in mind the different types of aircraft we've discussed in this section. Think about which ones excite you the most and imagine yourself at the controls, soaring through the skies and experiencing the thrill of flight.

In the sections ahead, we'll explore the steps you need to take to become a pilot, and you'll learn about the various paths you can choose in your flying career.

Whether you're drawn to the freedom of gliding, the precision of helicopter flight, or the power and speed of jet aircraft, there's a world of possibilities waiting for you in the realm of aviation.

As you learn more about the different types of aircraft and their uses, you'll also gain a greater appreciation for the incredible ingenuity and innovation that have driven the development of aviation over the years. From the simple gliders of Otto Lilienthal to the cutting-edge drones of today, each new aircraft represents a step forward in our quest to conquer the skies.

Remember, the sky is a vast and wondrous place, full of countless opportunities for adventure, discovery, and personal growth. No matter which type of aircraft you choose to pilot, always approach your flying with curiosity, passion, and a sense of wonder. By doing so, you'll not only become a skilled and confident pilot, but you'll also carry on the proud tradition of the aviation pioneers who came before you.

high-flying heroes - the role of pilots in society

From transporting people and goods to providing critical services, pilots make a huge difference in our daily lives. Are you ready to discover how pilots help shape the world around us? Let's dive in!

1. Connecting the world: One of the most significant ways pilots impact society is by connecting people and places across the globe. Commercial airline pilots transport millions of passengers every year, enabling us to visit faraway destinations, reunite with loved ones, and conduct business in different countries. In our increasingly interconnected world, pilots play a crucial role in bridging distances and bringing people together.

2. Delivering essential goods: Pilots are also responsible for transporting cargo, including food, medicine, and other essential supplies. From small bush planes delivering supplies to remote communities to massive cargo jets shipping goods across continents, pilots help ensure that people have access to the items they need to live and thrive.

3. Saving lives: Pilots play a vital role in emergency situations, using their skills to save lives and provide critical support. For example, medical pilots transport patients in need of urgent care, while search and rescue pilots locate and help people in distress. In times of natural disasters or humanitarian crises, pilots help deliver aid and evacuate those affected by the events.

4. Protecting our environment: Some pilots work in the field of environmental protection, using their unique perspective from the skies to monitor wildlife populations, track pollution, and even help fight forest

fires. By using their skills for environmental conservation, these pilots contribute to a healthier planet for all of us.

5. Defending our nations: Military pilots serve their countries by protecting national interests and maintaining peace and security. From air-to-air combat to intelligence gathering, military pilots play a key role in preserving our way of life.

6. Inspiring future generations: Pilots can serve as role models for young people, inspiring them to pursue their dreams and achieve their goals. By sharing their experiences and passion for aviation, pilots can encourage future generations to reach for the stars and believe in themselves.

7. Pushing the boundaries of exploration: Throughout history, pilots have played a central role in exploring our world and pushing the limits of human knowledge. From Charles Lindbergh's groundbreaking transatlantic flight to the daring exploits of astronauts like Neil Armstrong, pilots have helped us uncover new horizons and expand our understanding of the universe.

Now that we've explored some of the many ways pilots contribute to society, it's easy to see why they are often regarded as heroes. By using their skills and knowledge to help others, pilots make our world a better, safer, and more connected place.

As you continue on your journey to become a pilot, consider the positive impact you can have on the lives of others. Whether you choose to fly for a commercial airline, dedicate your career to saving lives, or even venture into the realm of space exploration, the possibilities are truly limitless.

Remember, as a pilot, you'll have the unique opportunity to touch the lives of countless people and make a lasting difference in the world. By approaching your career with a spirit of service and a commitment to excellence, you'll not only achieve personal success but also contribute to the greater good of society.

So, as you reach for the skies and follow in the footsteps of the remarkable pilots who came before you, know that you're not just chasing a dream – you're also embarking on a journey to make a real difference in the lives of others. With dedication, hard work, and a passion for flight, you have the power to become a high-flying hero and a positive force for change in our world.

As you progress through this book and gain a deeper understanding of the responsibilities and opportunities that come with being a pilot, keep the role of pilots in society in mind. You'll not only have the chance to explore the skies and experience the thrill of flight, but you'll also be part of a larger community of individuals who make our world a better place.

Whether you find yourself flying to new and exotic destinations, delivering essential supplies to those in need, or even helping to protect our planet, the sky truly is the limit for the impact you can have as a pilot. As you continue to learn, grow, and develop your skills, always remember that you have the power to make a difference and inspire others to do the same.

2 /
the path to
becoming a pilot

ready for takeoff - basic requirements to become a pilot

ARE you ready to start your journey toward becoming a pilot? Great! In this section, we'll talk about the basic requirements you need to meet in order to become a pilot. Don't worry, we'll guide you through each step, so you know exactly what you need to do to make your dream of flying a reality!

1. Age requirements: The first thing to consider is your age. To start flight training and work toward your pilot's license, you need to be at least 16 years old to solo and 17 years old to earn a private pilot's license. However, that doesn't mean you can't start learning about aviation before then! You can always begin

studying and exploring the world of flying while you're waiting to reach the minimum age.

2. Medical certificate: Before you can start flying, you'll need to obtain a medical certificate. This is a document issued by a certified Aviation Medical Examiner (AME) after you pass a physical examination. The medical certificate ensures that you're in good health and able to safely operate an aircraft. There are different classes of medical certificates, depending on the type of flying you plan to do, but for most new pilots, a third-class medical certificate is sufficient.

3. Education: While there's no specific educational requirement to become a pilot, having a strong foundation in math, science, and English can be very helpful in your training. Additionally, many flight schools and aviation programs require at least a high school diploma or equivalent. Don't worry if you're not quite there yet – you still have time to work on your education and prepare for your future in aviation!

4. Flight training: To become a pilot, you'll need to complete flight training at an approved flight school or with a certified flight instructor. During your training, you'll learn about the principles of flight, aircraft systems, navigation, and more. You'll also practice essential flying skills, such as takeoffs, landings, and emergency procedures. Flight training can be an

exciting and rewarding experience, so enjoy every moment!

5. Knowledge test: Before you can earn your pilot's license, you'll need to pass a written knowledge test. This exam covers a range of topics related to aviation, such as weather, regulations, and airspace. To prepare for the test, you can study on your own, take a ground school course, or work with a knowledgeable mentor. Remember, practice makes perfect – so don't be afraid to ask questions and seek help if you need it!

6. Practical test: Finally, once you've completed your flight training and passed the written knowledge test, you'll need to demonstrate your skills in a practical test, also known as a checkride. During the checkride, an examiner will observe your flying abilities and test your knowledge of aviation regulations and procedures. If you pass the checkride, congratulations – you'll officially be a licensed pilot!

Now that you know the basic requirements to become a pilot, you might be wondering how long it takes to achieve your goal. The answer depends on a variety of factors, such as your availability, your flight school's schedule, and your personal learning pace. On average, it takes most people about 6 to 12 months to earn a private pilot's license. However, your journey doesn't end there – as a pilot, you'll always be learning and growing, so keep that passion for aviation alive!

As you embark on this exciting path, remember that becoming a pilot takes dedication, hard work, and a commitment to safety. By approaching your training with a positive attitude and a willingness to learn, you'll be well on your way to achieving your dream of soaring through the skies.

As you work toward meeting the basic requirements to become a pilot, always remember the importance of perseverance and staying focused on your goals. There will be challenges along the way, but with determination and a positive mindset, you can overcome any obstacle and make your dream of flying a reality.

Also, don't forget that becoming a pilot is about more than just earning your license. It's about joining a community of passionate individuals who share your love for aviation and who are dedicated to making a difference in the world. By supporting one another and learning from each other's experiences, you'll be part of a vibrant and diverse group of people who are committed to pursuing their dreams and making the skies a safer, more exciting place for all.

skyward bound – how to gain flight experience

Are you excited to take to the skies? Fantastic! In this section, we're going to explore how to gain flight experience – a crucial step in your journey to becoming a pilot. This is where you'll put what you've learned into practice, and truly start feeling like a pilot!

1. Flight School: Your flight journey will kick off with attending flight school. This is where you'll learn the ins and outs of flying an aircraft, under the guidance of an experienced flight instructor. Flight schools offer structured programs that include both ground school (classroom learning) and flight training (hands-on experience). You'll start with basic maneuvers and gradually progress to more complex operations, like navigating, flying at night, or even handling emergencies.

2. Flight Simulators: Flight simulators are an excellent tool for gaining flight experience without even leaving the ground! Simulators mimic the controls and operations of a real aircraft, making them a safe and cost-effective way to practice your flying skills. They allow you to experience different flight conditions and scenarios, like bad weather or engine failures, helping you prepare for real-life situations.

3. Student Pilot Solo Flights: Once your flight instructor feels you're ready, you'll have the thrilling opportunity to fly solo - that means flying an airplane all by yourself! This is a big milestone for every student pilot. During solo flights, you'll put into practice everything you've learned, gaining invaluable experience and confidence in your abilities.

4. Cross-Country Flights: As part of your training, you'll also take cross-country flights. These are flights that take you at least 50 nautical miles away from your starting airport. They'll help you gain experience in planning and navigating longer flights, and you'll learn how to communicate with different air traffic control towers. It's like a road trip, but in the sky!

5. Flight Clubs and Groups: Joining a flight club or group is another great way to gain flight experience. These clubs often offer opportunities to rent aircraft at lower rates, making it more affordable to accumulate flight hours. Plus, being part of a community of fellow aviation enthusiasts provides a fantastic support network and a chance to learn from others.

6. Volunteer Opportunities: Believe it or not, you can also gain flight experience while helping others! Some organizations offer volunteer pilot programs, where you can use your flying skills for a good cause, like transporting medical patients or delivering

supplies to remote areas. It's a win-win situation – you get to log more flight hours and make a positive impact!

7. Advanced Ratings and Certificates: Once you've earned your private pilot's license, there's still plenty to learn! You can pursue advanced ratings and certificates, like an instrument rating (which allows you to fly in lower visibility conditions) or a commercial pilot's license (which allows you to get paid to fly). Each new rating or certificate requires additional training and flight experience, providing more opportunities for you to hone your skills.

Gaining flight experience is an exciting part of your journey to becoming a pilot. It's where you'll see your knowledge and skills come to life, and where you'll learn to handle the challenges and rewards of flying an aircraft. Remember, every hour you spend in the sky is a step closer to your dream.

As we continue in the sections to come, we'll delve deeper into the specifics of flight training, and what you can expect as you work toward earning your pilot's license. Remember, becoming a skilled and confident pilot doesn't happen overnight – it takes time, patience, and a lot of practice. But with each flight, you'll grow more confident in your abilities and closer to achieving your goal.

So, are you ready to take off and gain some flight experience? If so, strap on your seatbelt and prepare for an incredible journey! You'll learn, grow, face challenges, and celebrate victories. Every moment you spend flying is another step closer to reaching your dream of becoming a pilot.

Moreover, gaining flight experience is not just about logging hours. It's about understanding the beauty and responsibility of flight, about feeling the joy of soaring above the clouds, and about learning to respect and navigate the challenges that come with being a pilot. It's about becoming a part of a community that shares your love for the skies and supports your journey every step of the way.

As you embark on this adventure, remember to enjoy the journey. Every flight is an opportunity to learn something new, to improve your skills, and to gain a deeper appreciation for the incredible world of aviation.

learning to fly – an overview of the learning process

Ready for takeoff? Great! In this section, we'll explore the learning process for becoming a pilot. This journey is filled with exciting discoveries, new skills, and a whole lot of fun. So, let's dive in!

1. Ground School: Before you can take to the skies, you'll start your journey on the ground. Ground school is a classroom-style learning environment where you'll study the theory of flight, navigation, meteorology, and aviation law. You'll learn how airplanes work, how to read maps and weather reports, and the rules you need to follow when you're flying. It might sound like a lot, but don't worry, your instructor will guide you through it all.

2. Flight Lessons: Now, here's where things really start to take off! Once you've got the basics down, you'll start your flight lessons. This is where you'll learn to control an aircraft under the guidance of an experienced flight instructor. You'll start with basic maneuvers, like climbing, descending, and turning. As you progress, you'll learn more complex skills, like taking off, landing, and even handling emergencies.

3. Solo Flights: After your instructor feels you're ready, you'll get to experience the thrill of your first solo flight. That's right, you'll be the one in control, flying the airplane all by yourself! Solo flights are an incredible milestone in your journey and a great way to gain confidence in your abilities.

4. Cross-Country Flights: As part of your training, you'll also embark on cross-country flights, where you'll fly to an airport at least 50 nautical miles away from your home base. These flights will help you gain

experience in planning and navigating longer journeys and communicating with different air traffic control towers. It's a big adventure in the big blue sky!

5. Check Rides: After completing all your flight training, it's time for the final test, known as a check-ride. This is a practical exam where you'll demonstrate your flying skills and knowledge to an examiner. It's your chance to show everything you've learned and earn your pilot's license.

6. Continuing Education: Even after you earn your license, your learning doesn't stop. The world of aviation is always evolving, and there are always new things to learn. Whether it's earning advanced ratings, attending safety seminars, or just practicing your skills, continuing education is a key part of being a responsible and proficient pilot.

The learning process to become a pilot is a journey, filled with challenges, rewards, and a lot of excitement. Each step brings you closer to your dream of flying and offers new opportunities to grow and learn. It's a process that requires patience, dedication, and a love of learning.

As we move forward in this book, we'll delve deeper into the details of flight training, explore the different career paths in aviation, and share tips and advice to help you on your journey. Remember, the path to becoming a pilot is not always easy, but it's certainly worth it. With every challenge you overcome, you'll become a more skilled and confident pilot, ready to take on the skies.

3 /
pilot training and education

ground school - your first step to the skies

BEFORE WE CAN GLIDE through the clouds, we have to build a strong foundation on the ground. Yes, you guessed it, we're talking about ground school, your first step in your journey to becoming a pilot. But what exactly is ground school, you ask? Let's find out!

1. What is Ground School?: Ground school is like your regular school, but with a twist. Instead of learning about math or history, you'll be learning about aviation. It's where you'll understand the theory behind flying before you hop into an airplane. It's a crucial

part of your training, setting the base for all the fun and learning that's about to come.

2. The Aviation Classroom: The ground school classes are held in a classroom setting, often right at the airport! Your instructor will guide you through the lessons, which will include a mix of lectures, discussions, and even computer-based training. The classroom setting allows you to ask questions, interact with your peers, and learn from others' experiences. It's a community where everyone shares the same passion - flying!

3. Subjects You'll Learn: Now, let's talk about what you'll learn in ground school. You'll dive into the principles of flight (how an airplane flies), learn about different aircraft systems, study weather and how it impacts flying, and understand navigation techniques. You'll also study aviation regulations to make sure you're always following the rules of the sky. It might sound complex, but don't worry! It's all part of the adventure, and your instructors will make sure you understand each concept thoroughly.

. . .

4. Applying What You Learn: One of the best parts about ground school is that you get to apply what you learn almost immediately. As you move from ground school to your flight lessons, you'll see how the theories you learned in class work in real life. It's incredibly exciting to see your classroom knowledge come to life when you're up in the sky!

5. Preparing for the Written Exam: Ground school also helps you prepare for the written exam you'll need to pass to earn your pilot's license. This exam tests your knowledge of the subjects you learned in ground school. Don't worry though, with all the studying you'll be doing, you'll be well prepared to ace this exam!

6. Fun and Games: Ground school isn't just about studying. It's also about having fun! You'll participate in engaging activities and games that make learning interesting and exciting. It's a unique experience that combines learning with a whole lot of fun.

Ground school is an exciting part of your journey to becoming a pilot. It's a place where you'll learn, grow, and start your adventure in the world of aviation. While it might seem challenging at times, remember, every great pilot started right where you are now. With patience, dedication, and a sense of curiosity, you'll conquer this phase of your training and be one step closer to your dream of flying.

flight school - your gateway to the skies

After conquering ground school, it's time to take a thrilling leap towards our dream of flying. Where, you ask? Flight school, of course! This is where we get our hands on the controls and our feet off the ground. Ready to learn more? Let's take flight!

1. What is Flight School?: Flight school is the exciting part of your pilot training where you'll actually learn to fly an aircraft. It's an adventure that happens in the air under the guidance of a certified flight instructor. You'll be learning, practicing, and perfecting your flying skills in real-time!

2. The Flight Training Aircraft: Your lessons will take place in a training aircraft, a special kind of plane designed for learning pilots. It's smaller than the

commercial planes you might have seen, but it's perfectly equipped to help you learn everything you need to know about flying. It will be your learning partner in this exciting journey!

3. Your Flight Instructor: Guiding you through this journey will be your flight instructor, an experienced pilot who's there to teach you, guide you, and ensure your safety. They'll be by your side, sharing their knowledge, answering your questions, and cheering you on every step of the way.

4. From Pre-flight to Post-flight: Each flight lesson follows a sequence. First, you'll perform a pre-flight check, where you'll inspect the aircraft to make sure it's ready to fly. Then, with your instructor, you'll fly the planned lesson, practicing maneuvers and navigation. After landing, you'll debrief, discussing what you did well and what you can improve for next time. Every part of this process is a learning opportunity!

5. Skills You'll Learn: Now, let's talk about what you'll learn in flight school. You'll start with basic maneuvers, like straight and level flight, climbing, descending, and

turning. You'll learn to take off and land, navigate, and communicate with air traffic control. As you progress, you'll handle more complex tasks, like flying in different weather conditions, dealing with simulated emergencies, and even flying at night!

6. First Solo Flight: One of the most memorable moments in flight school is your first solo flight. When your instructor feels you're ready, they'll step out of the plane, and you'll take off all by yourself! It's an exciting milestone that marks your growth as a pilot.

7. Progress Checks: Throughout flight school, you'll have progress checks to ensure you're ready to move on to the next level. These checks are like mini-tests where another instructor will observe your flying skills. It's a great way to show off what you've learned!

Flight school is an adventure that brings your dream of flying to life. It's a journey that challenges you, rewards you, and fills you with a sense of accomplishment. Remember, every flight is a step closer to your goal. Embrace the learning, cherish the experiences, and always keep your spirits soaring high.

passing the faa written and practical exams – your path to official pilot status

After all that learning, practicing, and flying, it's time to face the final challenges on your path to becoming a pilot: the FAA written and practical exams. Don't worry! With all the knowledge and skills you've gained, you're more than ready. Let's dive into what these exams are all about!

1. Understanding the FAA Exams: The FAA, or Federal Aviation Administration, is the organization in charge of aviation in the United States. They set the standards for pilots, and their exams are the final hurdles you'll need to clear. The written exam tests your knowledge of aviation theory, while the practical exam, also known as the checkride, tests your flying skills.

2. Preparing for the Written Exam: Remember all those subjects you studied in ground school? They come into play here. The written exam covers topics like aircraft systems, weather, navigation, and aviation regulations. It's a multiple-choice test, and you'll need to score at least 70% to pass. Your ground school training has

prepared you well, and with some dedicated study time, you'll be ready to ace this exam.

3. The Day of the Written Exam: On exam day, make sure you're well-rested and have a good breakfast. Take your time, read each question carefully, and trust your knowledge. Remember, it's okay to be a little nervous. That's just your excitement showing!

4. Preparing for the Checkride: The checkride is your opportunity to show what a skilled pilot you've become. It consists of two parts: an oral exam where you'll answer questions about flying, and a flight test where you'll demonstrate your skills in the air. It might sound a bit intimidating, but remember, every lesson in flight school has been preparing you for this day.

5. The Day of the Checkride: On the day of your checkride, arrive early to prepare your aircraft and review your flight plan. During the test, stay calm, communicate clearly with your examiner, and, most importantly, fly the plane safely. If you make a mistake, don't worry! Just correct it and move on. Your ability to handle mistakes is part of being a good pilot.

. . .

6. Celebrating Your Success: Once you've passed these exams, it's time to celebrate! You've earned your pilot's license, and the sky is truly yours to explore. It's a moment of immense pride and joy, a testament to your hard work, dedication, and passion for flying.

Facing the FAA exams can feel like standing on the runway, ready for takeoff. It's a mix of anticipation, excitement, and a touch of nerves. But remember, every pilot who has soared through the skies has stood where you're standing. With preparation, determination, and a love for flying, you'll clear these final hurdles and embrace the incredible journey that awaits you.

4 /
exploring different aviation careers

commercial airline pilot - sky-high careers

NOW THAT WE'VE cleared the runway and are airborne with our pilot's licenses, let's aim for the next horizon: becoming a commercial airline pilot. It's a career filled with responsibility, adventure, and the opportunity to connect people and places across our vast world. Let's buckle up and learn more about it!

1. What is a Commercial Airline Pilot?: A commercial airline pilot is someone who flies passenger planes for an airline. They might fly people on vacation, business travelers, or even other pilots! Every time you've been on an airplane, there was a commercial airline pilot at the controls.

2. The Job of an Airline Pilot: An airline pilot's job

involves more than just flying the plane. They check the aircraft to make sure it's safe, plan the flight path, communicate with air traffic control, and handle any unexpected situations. And of course, they get to soar through the skies, navigating the airplane to its destination.

3. Becoming an Airline Pilot: To become an airline pilot, you'll need to gain more flight experience, usually by flying smaller planes or working as a flight instructor. Then, you'll need to earn your airline transport pilot (ATP) certificate, which requires passing another FAA exam and meeting minimum flight hours. The journey may be long, but the view from the cockpit of an airliner is worth it!

4. Life as an Airline Pilot: Airline pilots often travel a lot, spending time in different cities and even different countries. They work with a crew of other pilots, flight attendants, and ground staff to ensure every flight is safe and comfortable. It's a job that offers new experiences and views every day!

5. The Rewards of Being an Airline Pilot: Besides the excitement of flying, airline pilots also get the satisfaction of connecting people with the places and people they love. They get to see the world from above, witness beautiful sunrises and sunsets, and enjoy the camaraderie of their fellow crew members. Plus, they inspire future generations of pilots, just like you!

6. The Responsibility of an Airline Pilot: As thrilling as the job is, it also comes with great responsibility. Airline pilots are responsible for the safety of their passengers and crew, the smooth operation of the flight, and the expensive aircraft they command. It's a job that requires focus, precision, and dedication.

Embarking on a career as a commercial airline pilot is like setting course for a distant destination. It's a journey filled with learning, growing, and reaching new heights. Remember, becoming a pilot is not just about flying; it's about embracing a lifestyle of adventure, responsibility, and the joy of connecting people and places.

corporate or charter pilot - charting your unique path

We've taken a look at commercial airline pilots, the folks flying the big jets you see at major airports. Now, let's discover another exciting avenue for pilots: corporate and charter aviation. These pilots fly differently, offering a unique experience and a distinct career path. Ready to explore? Let's go!

1. What is a Corporate or Charter Pilot?: A corporate pilot flies company aircraft for business purposes, taking executives to meetings, factories, or other destinations. A charter pilot, on the other hand, flies private

passengers who have rented the aircraft for a specific trip. In both cases, pilots get to fly a variety of aircraft, often smaller than those used by airlines, but no less thrilling!

2. The Job of a Corporate or Charter Pilot: Corporate and charter pilots plan their flights, check their aircraft for safety, and then fly to their destination, just like airline pilots. However, their schedules can be more flexible, with flights often determined by the needs of the passengers. This can mean flying to airports that airlines don't serve, providing a unique challenge and variety.

3. Becoming a Corporate or Charter Pilot: To become a corporate or charter pilot, you'll need your pilot's license and usually a certain number of flight hours. Some pilots gain these hours through instructing or other flying jobs. Then, you might need specific training for the type of aircraft you'll be flying. Every step is an adventure, adding to your skills and experiences as a pilot.

4. Life as a Corporate or Charter Pilot: Life as a corporate or charter pilot can be varied and exciting. One day, you might be flying a team of executives to a business meeting; the next, you could be whisking a family off on their dream vacation. You may have the chance to explore places far off the beaten track, experiencing a range of cultures and landscapes.

5. The Rewards of Being a Corporate or Charter Pilot: One of the main rewards is the variety. Every day can bring a new destination, a new challenge, and new people to meet. You'll also have the satisfaction of providing a valuable service, helping people reach their destinations efficiently and comfortably.

6. The Responsibility of a Corporate or Charter Pilot: Like all pilots, corporate and charter pilots have a responsibility to ensure the safety of their passengers and their aircraft. They also need to provide a high level of service, as their passengers might be paying a premium for a private flight. It's a job that requires both skill in the cockpit and attention to passenger needs.

Choosing a career as a corporate or charter pilot is like choosing to explore the less-traveled skies. It's a career that offers variety, challenge, and the opportunity to provide a unique service. Remember, being a pilot is not just about how you fly, but also who you fly for and where you fly to.

military pilot - flying for freedom

We've explored the world of commercial, corporate, and charter pilots, but there's another thrilling path for those daring and disciplined enough: becoming a military pilot. This section is all about the brave men and women who fly in the service of their country. Ready for takeoff? Let's jet!

1. What is a Military Pilot?: A military pilot is a member of the armed forces who flies aircraft for defense, rescue missions, reconnaissance, and sometimes combat. They can fly a variety of aircraft, from fighter jets to large transport planes, and even helicopters.

2. The Job of a Military Pilot: Military pilots have a wide range of duties. They might patrol the skies, carry troops or supplies, perform search and rescue operations, or engage in combat missions. Whatever their specific role, all military pilots contribute to their country's defense and humanitarian efforts.

3. Becoming a Military Pilot: To become a military pilot, you'll need to join the armed forces and complete rigorous training programs, including military flight school. It's a challenging path that requires physical fitness, mental toughness, and a strong commitment to serving your country.

4. Life as a Military Pilot: Life as a military pilot can be challenging but also incredibly rewarding. You might be stationed at bases around the world, participate in vital missions, and work with a team of dedicated professionals. It's a career that demands the best from you, but also offers unique experiences and a strong sense of purpose.

5. The Rewards of Being a Military Pilot: Besides the thrill of flying some of the world's most advanced aircraft, military pilots also experience the honor of serving their country. They are part of a proud tradition, and their work can make a real difference in the world, whether defending their nation or helping people in need.

6. The Responsibility of a Military Pilot: Military pilots carry a great deal of responsibility. They are entrusted with expensive equipment, critical missions, and often, the lives of others. It's a role that requires discipline, courage, and a deep sense of duty.

Choosing to become a military pilot is a significant decision, one that involves not just a career, but a commitment to a way of life. It's a path that can be challenging, but also deeply fulfilling, offering the chance to serve, to grow, and to fly like few others do.

flight instructor - guiding the next generation of flyers

We've journeyed through various avenues of being a pilot, haven't we? From commercial to military aviation, each path has its unique thrills and challenges. Now, let's explore a different path, one that allows you to share the joy of flying with others - becoming a flight instructor. Buckle up, and let's dive in!

1. What is a Flight Instructor?: A flight instructor is a certified, experienced pilot who teaches others how to fly. They guide student pilots, helping them understand the principles of flight, master the controls of an aircraft, and gain the skills and confidence they need to soar on their own.

2. The Job of a Flight Instructor: Flight instructors teach a wide range of skills. They help students understand flight theory in a classroom setting, then apply that theory in the cockpit. From basic takeoffs and landings to complex maneuvers and emergency procedures, flight instructors guide their students every step of the way.

3. Becoming a Flight Instructor: To become a flight instructor, you'll need a commercial pilot's license, a flight instructor certificate, and a strong foundation of flying experience. You'll also need to have a good understanding of teaching methods because it's not just about knowing how to fly, but also how to effectively pass that knowledge onto others.

4. Life as a Flight Instructor: Life as a flight instructor can be incredibly rewarding. You'll spend your days in the cockpit, sharing your love of flying with eager students. Each day brings new challenges as you adapt your teaching to meet the unique needs of each student.

5. The Rewards of Being a Flight Instructor: One of the greatest rewards of being a flight instructor is seeing your students grow. There's nothing quite like the moment a student pilot takes off or lands for the first time, their face glowing with pride and excitement. As a flight instructor, you get to be a part of these incredible moments.

6. The Responsibility of a Flight Instructor: Being a flight instructor comes with a great deal of responsibility. You're not only in charge of your own safety, but also the safety of your student. It's your job to ensure they are prepared for each flight and to guide them through any challenges they might encounter.

Choosing to become a flight instructor means choosing to inspire, to educate, and to share the joy of flight. It's a career that requires patience, knowledge, and a passion for teaching. Remember, as a flight instructor, you're not just teaching students to fly— you're helping them to achieve their dreams.

air traffic controller - master of the skies

We've shared many adventures in the world of aviation, haven't we? Each section has taken us closer to finding your perfect place in the wide, blue yonder. Now, let's explore a path that keeps the sky organized and safe, one that's as vital as it is fascinating: the air traffic controller. Let's lift off!

1. What is an Air Traffic Controller?: An air traffic controller is a person who manages the flow of aircraft in the sky and on the ground. They make sure planes take off and land safely, help pilots navigate through busy airspaces, and coordinate the movements of multiple aircraft at once.

2. The Job of an Air Traffic Controller: Air traffic controllers keep an eye on multiple planes at the same time, communicating with pilots to give them instructions about their flight path, altitude, and speed. They work in control towers at airports, in radar centers, and in area control centers. It's a job that requires extreme focus and quick decision-making skills.

3. Becoming an Air Traffic Controller: To become an air traffic controller, you'll need to complete a specialized training program and pass a series of exams. These programs focus on things like aviation safety, airspace management, and communication skills. It's a challenging path, but one that leads to an exciting career.

4. Life as an Air Traffic Controller: Being an air traffic controller means staying alert and focused. Each day is filled with new challenges as weather conditions change, flight schedules shift, and unexpected situa-

tions arise. It's a role that requires precision, quick thinking, and a cool head under pressure.

5. The Rewards of Being an Air Traffic Controller: One of the great rewards of being an air traffic controller is knowing that you're helping to keep the skies safe. Every time a plane takes off or lands safely, it's partly thanks to the work of air traffic controllers. It's a job that makes a real difference.

6. The Responsibility of an Air Traffic Controller: With great power comes great responsibility. Air traffic controllers are responsible for the safety of thousands of people every day. They need to make quick, accurate decisions to ensure that every flight arrives safely at its destination.

Choosing to become an air traffic controller is choosing a career of responsibility, precision, and adrenaline. It's a path that offers a unique perspective on the world of aviation, one where you can truly make a difference.

aircraft mechanic - the wizards behind the wings

Our journey into the world of aviation continues, and with each section, we uncover a new and fascinating path. Today, we'll delve into a role that's all about keeping aircraft flying high and safe: the aircraft mechanic. Fasten your safety belts, and let's take off!

1. What is an Aircraft Mechanic?: An aircraft mechanic, sometimes also called an aviation maintenance technician, is a skilled professional who ensures that aircraft are in perfect flying condition. They inspect, repair, and maintain all parts of an aircraft, from the engine to the landing gear, and everything in between.

2. The Job of an Aircraft Mechanic: Aircraft mechanics do a lot more than just fix planes. They conduct regular inspections, diagnose issues, replace parts, and even perform tests to make sure everything's working as it should. It's a bit like being a detective, a problem-solver, and a wizard all in one!

3. Becoming an Aircraft Mechanic: To become an aircraft mechanic, you'll need to attend a technical school or training program that focuses on aviation maintenance. These programs teach you about the different parts of an aircraft, how they work, and how to repair them. Once you've completed your training, you'll need to pass a series of exams to get your aircraft mechanic certification.

4. Life as an Aircraft Mechanic: As an aircraft mechanic, no two days are the same. One day, you might be repairing a jet engine, the next you could be conducting a routine inspection on a helicopter. It's a

job that requires a sharp mind, a steady hand, and a keen eye for detail.

5. The Rewards of Being an Aircraft Mechanic: There's a great sense of satisfaction that comes from knowing you've helped keep an aircraft safe and ready for flight. Plus, you get to work with some of the most advanced technology in the world, and you'll never stop learning new things.

6. The Responsibility of an Aircraft Mechanic: As an aircraft mechanic, you hold a crucial responsibility. Your work ensures the safety of every passenger and crew member aboard each flight. Your thorough inspections and meticulous repairs help keep the skies safe for everyone.

Choosing to become an aircraft mechanic means choosing a career where your skills and knowledge have a direct impact on the safety and efficiency of air travel. It's a role that combines technical know-how, problem-solving, and a genuine love for aviation.

5 /
life as a pilot

the daily routine of a pilot - a day in the sky

WE'VE LEARNED about many facets of aviation, haven't we? We've looked at various roles, from aircraft mechanics to air traffic controllers, but now let's take a closer look at the life of a pilot. What's a day in the life of a pilot like? Let's find out!

1. Early Morning: A pilot's day starts early. Before the sun rises, pilots are up and getting ready for the day. They need to be alert and ready for whatever the day brings, so a good night's sleep and a healthy breakfast are musts!

2. Pre-flight Briefing: Once they arrive at the airport, pilots attend a pre-flight briefing. This meeting includes the pilots, co-pilots, and sometimes flight

attendants. They discuss the flight plan, weather conditions, and any potential issues. It's a bit like a team huddle before a big game!

3. Pre-flight Checks: After the briefing, it's time for pre-flight checks. This is when the pilot and co-pilot inspect the aircraft. They check the aircraft's exterior, the cockpit, and ensure all the systems are working correctly. This is a critical step to ensure everyone's safety.

4. Takeoff: With everything checked and ready, it's time for takeoff. The pilot communicates with air traffic control, pushes the throttle, and before you know it, the plane lifts off the ground. It's a moment that never loses its thrill!

5. In-Flight: Once in the air, pilots monitor the aircraft's systems and navigate the plane. They stay in contact with air traffic control, adjust the plane's course as needed, and respond to any unexpected events.

6. Landing: As the journey nears its end, pilots prepare for landing. They communicate with air traffic control, align the plane with the runway, and guide the plane gently back to earth. It requires focus, precision, and a calm demeanor.

7. Post-Flight Duties: After landing, pilots have a few more tasks. They need to fill out logs and reports about the flight, check the aircraft once more, and then, at last, their workday comes to an end.

8. Rest and Repeat: After a long day, rest is crucial. Pilots need a clear mind for their duties, so getting enough sleep is very important. Then, the next day, they do it all over again!

Being a pilot is more than just flying a plane. It's about ensuring the safety of all onboard, staying calm under pressure, and making decisions that can make all the difference. It's a challenging job, but for those who love the thrill of flight, it's the best job in the world.

Remember, a pilot's day is filled with responsibilities, but it's also filled with incredible views and the unmatched feeling of soaring through the sky. So, future pilots, are you ready to take on the challenge and experience the thrill of flight every day? Your journey is just beginning, and the sky is waiting!

the importance of safety and professionalism - taking flight responsibly

Are you ready to dive into one of the most important aspects of being a pilot? I sure hope so, because today we're talking about safety and professionalism. These two elements are key in the cockpit, and they ensure that every flight is a successful one.

Safety is, without a doubt, the number one priority

in aviation. When you step into the cockpit, you're not just in control of a plane; you're also responsible for the lives of your passengers and crew. That's a big responsibility, but don't worry! As you learn and grow, you'll be equipped with the knowledge and skills to handle this task.

1. Safety First: The rules in aviation exist to keep everyone safe. Every procedure, every check, and every guideline has been put in place with safety in mind. As a pilot, it's crucial that you follow these rules to the letter. Always remember, safety first!

2. Constant Learning: In aviation, learning never stops. There are always new safety procedures, technologies, and regulations to keep up with. A good pilot is a lifelong learner, always ready to absorb new information to improve their skills and keep their passengers safe.

3. Emergency Situations: Part of being a safe pilot is knowing how to handle emergencies. Despite all precautions, unexpected situations can arise. That's why pilots train for various emergency scenarios, from engine failures to sudden weather changes. Being prepared for these situations is a key part of a pilot's job.

Professionalism, on the other hand, is all about how you conduct yourself as a pilot. It's about being reliable, respectful, and responsible. It's about doing your job to the best of your ability, and always striving to do better. Let's take a closer look at what professionalism means in the world of aviation.

1. Responsibility: As a pilot, you have a lot of responsibility. You're entrusted with the safe transport of your passengers and crew, and it's your job to ensure their journey is a smooth one. This means showing up prepared and ready to do your job, every single day.

2. Respect: Respect is a big part of professionalism. This means respecting your colleagues, your passengers, and the rules of aviation. It's about treating everyone with kindness and understanding, and always doing the right thing.

3. Reliability: A good pilot is a reliable one. When you're in the cockpit, your team and your passengers are counting on you. By being reliable, you show that you're someone they can trust, which is incredibly important in the aviation industry.

4. Continuous Improvement: Finally, professionalism means always striving to be better. Whether it's improving your flying skills, learning new safety procedures, or finding ways to be more efficient, a professional pilot is always looking for ways to improve.

Remember, being a pilot isn't just about flying. It's about being a leader, a team player, and a role model. It's about being someone people can count on, and always putting safety first. That's what it means to be a pilot.

And here's a secret: safety and professionalism go hand in hand. When you're professional, you're more likely to follow safety rules and guidelines. And when you're safe, you're showing your professionalism. They're two sides of the same coin, and both are incredibly important in the world of aviation.

challenges and rewards of the career - the highs and lows of life in the sky

It's time for a heart-to-heart. You've learned a lot about what it takes to become a pilot, but now, let's talk about what it really feels like to have this amazing job. Just like any career, being a pilot has its challenges and rewards. These highs and lows are all part of the journey that makes being a pilot such a unique and rewarding profession.

Let's start with some of the challenges. These are the parts of the job that can be tough, but remember, overcoming obstacles is part of what makes the journey so rewarding!

1. Training: Becoming a pilot requires a lot of learning and practice. You'll spend hours studying, attending classes, and practicing your flying skills. This can be tough, but it's also an exciting part of the jour-

ney. You'll learn so much, and the skills you gain will be with you for life!

2. Responsibility: As a pilot, you're responsible for the safety of your passengers and crew. This is a big responsibility, and it can feel overwhelming at times. But it's also a great privilege. You're trusted with people's lives, and that's something to be proud of.

3. Irregular Schedule: Being a pilot often means having an irregular schedule. You might have early morning flights, late night flights, or flights on weekends and holidays. This can be challenging, especially when it means missing out on time with friends and family. But it's part of the job, and it's something most pilots learn to manage.

Now, let's talk about the rewards. These are the things that make all the challenges worth it. The things that make being a pilot such an amazing career!

1. Flying: There's nothing quite like the feeling of flying. When you're up in the air, piloting an airplane, it's an indescribable feeling of freedom and exhilaration. This is one of the biggest rewards of being a pilot - you get to do something you love, every single day.

2. Travel: As a pilot, you'll have the opportunity to travel all over the world. You'll see places most people only dream of, and you'll experience different cultures and meet interesting people along the way. It's an adventure that never gets old.

3. Making a Difference: As a pilot, you're not just flying planes. You're connecting people to their loved ones, helping them get to important events, and even saving lives in emergency situations. You're making a difference in the world, and that's something to be proud of.

4. Lifelong Learning: If you love learning, then being a pilot is the perfect job for you. There's always something new to learn in aviation, whether it's a new safety procedure, a new piece of technology, or a new destination. It's a career that keeps you on your toes and keeps your mind sharp.

There you have it, future aviators. Being a pilot is a journey filled with challenges and rewards. It's a path that requires hard work, dedication, and a love of learning. But it's also a path filled with incredible experiences, unforgettable moments, and the joy of doing something you truly love.

Remember, every challenge is an opportunity to grow, and every reward is a testament to your hard work and dedication. Embrace the journey, future pilots. The sky is waiting for you!

6 /
tips for aspiring pilots

join aviation clubs or organizations - finding your flight crew

HAVE you ever thought about joining an aviation club or organization? If you're passionate about flying and want to connect with others who share your love for the skies, joining an aviation club is a fantastic idea! But you may be wondering, "What exactly is an aviation club, and what can I gain from being a part of one?" Well, let's dive in and find out!

First off, let's talk about what an aviation club or organization is. These are groups of people who come together because they all share a common interest in aviation. Some clubs focus on specific areas, like model aircraft building, while others are more general and welcome anyone with a love for all things aviation.

There are clubs and organizations for pilots, aviation enthusiasts, airplane mechanics, air traffic controllers, and more!

You might find aviation clubs in your school, your community, or even online. Each club is different, offering various activities, events, and opportunities for learning. Some clubs might organize trips to aviation museums or air shows, while others may offer workshops, guest speakers, or flight training opportunities.

So why should you consider joining an aviation club or organization? There are so many benefits, but let's explore some of the main ones:

1. Learning Opportunities: Aviation clubs are packed with learning opportunities. You can learn from experienced members, participate in workshops or seminars, and even get hands-on experience with different types of aircraft. It's a fantastic way to deepen your understanding of aviation and acquire new skills.

2. Networking: Joining an aviation club is a great way to meet people who share your passion. You'll get to connect with people of all ages and backgrounds who love aviation just as much as you do. These could be your future colleagues or mentors!

3. Fun Activities: Aviation clubs are not just about learning; they're also about having fun! From model

airplane competitions to visits to air shows, there's always something exciting happening.

4. Career Guidance: If you're serious about a career in aviation, joining a club can give you invaluable insights. You can get advice from experienced members, learn about different career paths, and maybe even find internship or job opportunities.

5. Community: Lastly, and perhaps most importantly, joining an aviation club gives you a sense of community. You'll be part of a group of people who understand your love for aviation and support your dreams.

Now, let's talk about some specific clubs and organizations you might consider joining:

1. Young Eagles: This is a program by the Experimental Aircraft Association (EAA) that gives young people ages 8 to 17 the opportunity to go flying in a general aviation airplane. It's a great way to get a taste of what it's like to be a pilot!

2. Civil Air Patrol (CAP): This is a U.S. Air Force auxiliary organization that offers cadet programs for youth ages 12 to 21. Cadets learn about aviation, leadership, and emergency services, and can even get opportunities to fly!

3. Aviation Explorer Posts: These are local clubs associated with the Boy Scouts of America's Learning

for Life program. They offer opportunities to explore careers in aviation and gain hands-on experience.

4. Air League: In the UK, this is an organization for young people interested in aviation. They offer a range of activities including gliding and powered flight training.

5. Online Forums: If you can't find a local club, or if you just want to connect with more aviation enthusiasts, consider joining an online aviation forum or group. These communities can be found on websites like Reddit or in apps like Discord.

Whether you're an aspiring pilot, mechanic, air traffic controller, or just a big fan of airplanes, joining an aviation club can be a fantastic step in your journey. It's not just about what you learn or who you meet, but also about the experiences you gain and the memories you create.

Remember, aviation is more than just a hobby or a career; it's a community. By joining a club or organization, you'll become part of this amazing world. You'll make friends who understand why you look up every time an airplane flies overhead, and who share your dream of reaching for the stars.

So, how do you join an aviation club? The first step is to do some research. Look online or ask around to find out what clubs are available in your area. If you're in school, ask your teachers or guidance counselor if there are any aviation clubs you could join. If not, maybe you could start one!

Once you've found a club that interests you, reach out to them. Most clubs are always looking for new members and will be more than happy to tell you how to join. You might need to fill out an application or pay a membership fee. Some clubs may also have age restrictions or other requirements.

But don't be discouraged if you don't meet the requirements for a certain club or if there aren't any clubs in your area. There are plenty of other ways to learn about aviation and connect with other enthusiasts. You could visit aviation museums, go to air shows, read books about aviation, watch documentaries, or even take a flight lesson.

Finally, remember that being part of a club is about more than just showing up to meetings. It's about participating, getting involved, and contributing to the group. Don't be afraid to ask questions, share your ideas, or take on leadership roles. After all, the more you put into your club, the more you'll get out of it.

In the end, joining an aviation club or organization is about more than just learning about airplanes. It's about finding your passion, chasing your dreams, and becoming part of a community that shares your love for the sky.

So why not give it a try? Who knows, joining an

aviation club might just be the first step on your journey to the stars. Maybe one day, you'll be the one inspiring others to reach for the sky, just as you were inspired. The sky is not the limit; it's just the beginning, and your adventure is waiting. Just remember to keep looking up!

attend air shows and aviation museums

There's something utterly magical about air shows and aviation museums. They're places where you can see, touch, and even smell history, where you can learn about the amazing feats of engineering and bravery that have shaped our world. So, let's take a trip, shall we?

Imagine standing in a crowd, eyes fixed on the sky as an aerobatic team performs breathtaking maneuvers. The planes zoom overhead, leaving trails of smoke behind them. They swoop and dive, flip and spin, their engines roaring so loudly you can feel it in your chest. That's the thrill of an air show.

Air shows are not just about the spectacle, though. They're about inspiration, about sparking a love of aviation in people of all ages. And who knows, maybe it'll be at an air show that you decide you want to become a pilot.

Now, let's take a step back in time and visit an aviation museum. Here, you can walk among historic aircraft, from the earliest biplanes to the most advanced jets. You can learn about the pioneers of aviation, the brave men and women who dared to defy gravity and took to the skies. You can even climb into a cockpit and imagine what it must have been like to fly these incredible machines.

But these places are not just about the past; they're about the future, too. Many aviation museums offer educational programs and workshops, where you can learn about the science of flight or even try your hand at building a model airplane. These programs can be a great way to learn more about aviation and maybe even ignite a passion that could lead you to become a pilot.

Whether you're watching an air show or exploring a museum, it's important to take the time to talk to the people around you. You might meet pilots, engineers, or aviation enthusiasts who can share their knowledge and experiences with you. Who knows, you might even make a new friend or mentor.

But most importantly, remember to have fun. Yes, air shows and museums are great places to learn, but they're also places to dream. So let your imagination take flight. Imagine yourself soaring through the clouds, seeing the world from a whole new perspective. Feel the thrill of the takeoff, the joy of flight, the satisfaction of a perfect landing. Dream about the places you could go, the people you could meet, the adventures you could have.

Because that's what aviation is all about. It's about daring to dream, about reaching for the stars, about exploring the endless possibilities of the sky. So, go ahead, let your imagination take flight. Who knows where it might lead you?

So, if you ever have a chance to attend an air show or visit an aviation museum, take it. You never know what you might discover or who you might meet. You never know what spark might be ignited, what dream might take flight.

Remember, you're not just an observer at these events—you're a participant, a part of the great adventure of aviation. And who knows, maybe one day you'll be the one up there in the sky, performing daring maneuvers or piloting an incredible machine, inspiring the next generation of aviators. The sky's the limit, so keep dreaming, keep learning, and keep reaching for the stars.

read books and magazines about aviation

Imagine standing on a bustling airport runway, surrounded by the sounds of roaring engines and the sights of soaring planes. Now, picture the people in those planes, the ones controlling those engines, guiding those massive machines through the clouds. They're pilots and aviation professionals, and they have one of the coolest jobs in the world. Wouldn't it be amazing to meet them, to learn from them, to maybe even be one of them someday? That's what networking in the aviation world is all about.

Now, you might be thinking, "Networking? Isn't that something adults do at fancy business meetings?" Well, yes and no. Networking can happen anywhere, and it's not just for grown-ups. It's about meeting people, learning from them, and building relationships. And in the world of aviation, it's a fantastic way to fuel your passion for flight.

So, how do you network with pilots and aviation professionals? First, it's important to remember that these folks were once kids like you, with big dreams and a passion for flight. They love to share their experiences and knowledge with young, eager minds. So don't be shy! Ask questions, show your enthusiasm, and most importantly, listen and learn.

Attending air shows and aviation events is a great place to start. These events often have pilots and other aviation professionals in attendance. They're usually more than happy to chat about their experiences, answer questions, and give advice. Plus, it's a great opportunity to see different types of aircraft up close and in action.

Joining aviation clubs or organizations can also provide opportunities to meet and learn from aviation professionals. These organizations often host guest speakers, field trips, and other educational events. Plus, being part of a club gives you a community of fellow aviation enthusiasts to share your journey with.

Don't forget about the power of online networking. Many pilots and aviation professionals are active on social media, where they share their experiences, advice, and even some pretty cool pictures and videos. Just remember to always be respectful and professional online, just as you would be in person.

When networking, remember that it's not just about getting something; it's about building relationships. Show genuine interest in the people you meet, and respect their time and expertise. And don't forget to say thank you. A little appreciation goes a long way.

Networking can also help you explore different careers in aviation. Every pilot's journey is unique, and talking to different professionals can give you an idea of the many paths you could take. From commercial pilots to military aviators, flight instructors to air traffic controllers, there's a whole world of aviation careers out there.

Remember, networking isn't just a one-time thing.

It's an ongoing process of learning, building relationships, and growing your passion for aviation. So keep asking questions, keep exploring, and keep reaching for the stars.

In the grand scheme of things, networking is all about connecting, not just with professionals in the field, but also with the world of aviation itself. It's about becoming part of a community of people who share your love for the sky. And who knows? The connections you make today might just help you soar to new heights tomorrow.

network with pilots and aviation professionals

Picture this: You're in a group of other young people who share your fascination with planes and the sky. You're surrounded by all things aviation. The smell of jet fuel is in the air, and you can hear the sounds of engines humming in the distance. Welcome to aviation camp!

Aviation camps and workshops are fantastic opportunities to dive deeper into your passion for flying. They're special places where you can learn a lot, have fun, and make new friends who share your interests. But what exactly happens at these camps and workshops? Let's find out!

At an aviation camp, every day is a new adventure. Maybe you'll start the day by learning about the physics of flight - how airplanes manage to stay up in the sky. You might build and test your own model planes, learning about different aircraft designs and how they affect an airplane's performance.

In some camps, you might even get the chance to use flight simulators. These are computer systems that mimic the experience of flying an actual plane. With a real cockpit setup and realistic graphics, you'll get a taste of what it's like to be a pilot - minus the actual flying part, of course.

In addition to learning about flying, you'll also learn about other important aspects of aviation. This could include learning about weather and how it affects flights, understanding air traffic control, or even getting a closer look at how planes are maintained and repaired. Remember, aviation is not just about the pilots - it's a vast field with many exciting opportunities.

Workshops at aviation camps often involve hands-on activities. This might include assembling model planes, learning how to pre-flight check a real aircraft, or even mapping out a flight plan. The aim is to give you a practical understanding of aviation, not just theory.

One of the best parts about aviation camps is the

people you'll meet. You'll be surrounded by instructors who are passionate about aviation and excited to share their knowledge. Plus, you'll meet other kids who share your love for flying. These friendships can last long after the camp is over, and who knows, you might even end up flying together someday!

Now, you might be wondering, "How do I find an aviation camp or workshop?" A good place to start is the internet. Look for aviation camps near you, and check out their websites to see what activities they offer. You can also ask your school counselor, local aviation clubs, or even pilots if they know of any good programs.

Remember, the goal of attending an aviation camp or workshop is not just to learn about flying, but to immerse yourself in the wonderful world of aviation. It's a chance to fuel your passion, gain new skills, and make lasting memories. So, whether you're building a model plane, sitting in a flight simulator, or just chatting with your new friends about your favorite aircraft, remember to enjoy every moment.

Aviation camps and workshops are more than just a fun summer activity. They're stepping stones on your journey into the world of aviation. The knowledge you gain, the experiences you have, and the friends you make could be the start of your very own aviation story. So pack your enthusiasm, fasten your seatbelt, and get ready for a thrilling adventure. The world of aviation is waiting for you!

participate in aviation camps and workshops

I bet you've heard the phrase "the sky's the limit" quite a few times, right? Well, in aviation, the sky isn't just the limit; it's the goal. It's a vast, beautiful, and awe-inspiring place where dreams take flight—quite literally!

If you're reading this, chances are you've already fallen in love with the idea of soaring among the clouds. You might be dreaming about the thrill of being a pilot, the satisfaction of maintaining airplanes as an aircraft mechanic, or the intellectual challenge of being an air traffic controller. Whatever your dream might be, I want you to remember one thing: dreams don't just happen. They require passion, hard work, dedication, and a pinch of courage.

Think about the Wright Brothers. They weren't just inventors who built the first successful airplane; they were dreamers who worked tirelessly, faced countless failures, and yet never gave up on their dream of powered flight. Their determination, combined with their hard work, changed the world forever.

Now, does that mean achieving your dreams will be

easy? Not necessarily. Any worthwhile goal requires effort. You might face obstacles and setbacks along the way. There might be times when you might even question if it's all worth it. In those moments, I want you to remember why you fell in love with aviation in the first place. Remember the feeling of excitement when you see a plane soaring high in the sky, the fascination with how such a massive machine can fly, and the dream of one day being part of this amazing world. Hold on to that passion, and use it as fuel to keep going.

Hard work doesn't mean you have to do everything alone, though. Reach out to others who share your interest. Remember those aviation clubs and organizations we talked about? They're filled with people who were once in your shoes, and they can provide invaluable support and guidance. Don't be afraid to ask for help, to learn from others, and to share your own experiences. After all, flying is a team effort.

Another important aspect of hard work is education. Learn as much as you can about aviation. Read books, attend workshops, visit museums, and take every opportunity to expand your knowledge. The more you know, the better prepared you'll be to face the challenges ahead.

And finally, don't forget to have fun along the way. While it's important to work hard and stay focused on your goal, it's also important to enjoy the journey. Celebrate your achievements, no matter how small. Take time to appreciate the beauty and wonder of flight. After all, love for aviation is what started you on this journey, and it's what will keep you going.

In the end, remember this: Your dreams are like an airplane. They might require a lot of work and preparation to get off the ground, but once they take flight, they can take you to amazing places. So, whether your dream is to fly a plane, fix a plane, or control the air traffic, keep working hard, stay focused, and never stop believing in yourself. The sky is waiting for you!

7 /
conclusion

encouragement to follow dreams and work hard

LET'S take a moment to think about the sky. It's enormous, isn't it? It stretches all around us in every direction, from the horizon that we see when we look straight ahead, to the vast space overhead that's full of clouds during the day and stars at night. It's so big, it can make you feel small. But here's the exciting part: that vast, wide-open sky is also full of endless possibilities, especially when it comes to aviation.

Now, you might be wondering, "What do you mean by endless possibilities?" Well, when you look at the sky, you see space, right? But when pilots, air traffic controllers, aircraft mechanics, and other aviation professionals look at the sky, they see opportunities, careers, adventures, and even dreams coming true.

Let's start with the obvious: pilots. When we think of aviation, pilots are often the first people that come to mind. And for a good reason! They get to fly the aircraft, navigate the skies, and take people and goods from one place to another. It's a job that requires skill, knowledge, and a lot of responsibility, but it also offers the thrill of flying and the chance to see the world from above. Plus, there are many types of pilots, from commercial airline pilots to cargo pilots, from private jet pilots to helicopter pilots. The possibilities are indeed endless!

But pilots aren't the only ones in aviation with a bird's eye view. There are also drone operators who control unmanned aircraft, which are used for everything from delivering packages to taking aerial photos. And let's not forget about astronauts who take the concept of flying to a whole new level: space!

Of course, aircraft need to be maintained, repaired, and kept in top shape to fly safely. That's where aircraft mechanics come in. They get to work with their hands, solving problems and fixing things. They also get to learn about the fascinating technology that makes flight possible.

And have you thought about the people who design aircraft? Aerospace engineers use their creativity and understanding of physics to design everything from airplanes to helicopters, from drones to rockets. If you love solving problems and designing things, this could be the job for you!

Now, let's talk about the people who keep everything organized: air traffic controllers. They manage the flow of aircraft in and out of airports and in the sky, making sure that everyone stays safe. It's a job that requires concentration, quick decision-making, and excellent communication skills. But for those who love a good challenge, it can be a perfect fit.

There's also a whole world of other careers in aviation that you might not have thought about. For example, did you know that some people specialize in rescuing people with helicopters in difficult-to-reach places? Or that others work to protect our environment by studying how aviation impacts climate change? And let's not forget about the flight attendants who ensure passengers have a comfortable and safe flight.

The truth is, there are as many possibilities in aviation as there are stars in the sky. Whether you want to fly a plane, design one, fix one, control one, or even just help people enjoy their flight, there's a place for you in aviation.

Remember, each one of these careers starts with a dream, a passion for flight, and the sky. So, next time you look up at the sky, think about the endless possibilities waiting for you. Then, spread your wings and prepare to soar, because the sky is not the limit; it's just the beginning!

the endless possibilities in aviation

Have you ever watched a bird soaring high in the sky, floating on the air currents, darting this way and that, and wondered what it must be like? Imagine the feeling of freedom, the exhilaration of speed, the breathtaking views. That, my friends, is the joy and excitement of flying!

When you're in the cockpit of an airplane, the world looks different. Everything is smaller, more compact. The houses look like tiny toy models, and the cars seem like they're moving in slow motion. You can see things that are hidden when you're on the ground, like the pattern of fields and forests, or the way rivers snake through the landscape. It's like being part of a giant, living map.

And the feeling! Oh, the feeling is indescribable. There's the thrill when the engines roar to life, and you feel the power of the aircraft beneath you. There's the moment of suspense as you speed down the runway, faster and faster until the wheels gently lift off the ground, and you're flying!

You might think that once you're in the air, it's a

smooth and calm ride, but that's not always the case. Just like driving a car, flying an airplane requires constant attention and adjustment. You have to keep an eye on the weather, watch out for other aircraft, and navigate your way to your destination. But don't worry, all these tasks add to the excitement and keep you on your toes.

Now, let's talk about the moment when you take the controls for the first time. It's a bit nerve-wracking, right? But it's also one of the most exhilarating feelings you'll ever experience. You're not just a passenger; you're the pilot! You have control over this powerful machine, and you can guide it through the sky. It's a feeling of accomplishment, of mastery, and it's absolutely amazing.

Flying isn't just about the destination; it's about the journey. It's about watching the sunrise from above the clouds, or seeing a city light up as the sun sets. It's about the peace and tranquility that come when you're high above the hustle and bustle of the world below. It's about the thrill of navigating through a thunderstorm, or the challenge of landing in strong winds. Every flight is a new adventure.

There are also the friendships and camaraderie that come with being a part of the aviation community. Whether it's the bond between pilot and co-pilot, the shared experiences with other students at flight school, or the friendships formed at air shows and aviation clubs, these relationships add another layer of joy to the experience of flying.

But perhaps the most exciting thing about flying is that it's a dream come true. Many people look up at the sky, watch the airplanes soaring above, and wish they could be up there too. And when you're in the cockpit, looking down at the world below, you realize that you've made that dream a reality. You're not just watching the birds; you're flying with them!

Sure, there will be challenges along the way. There will be times when the weather isn't perfect, or when the airplane doesn't behave the way you expect. But these challenges are part of the journey, part of the adventure. And when you overcome them, you'll feel a sense of accomplishment that's better than any smooth flight.

So, the next time you look up at the sky, think about the joy and excitement of flying. Imagine the thrill of taking off, the beauty of the world from above, the challenges and the triumphs. And remember, this can be your reality. With hard work, determination, and a passion for flight, you too can experience the joy and excitement of flying. Because in the end, there's really nothing quite like it.

Now, imagine this. It's early in the morning, the sun just beginning to peek over the horizon, painting the sky in shades of pink and orange. You're in the cockpit of an airplane, engine humming softly, and in front of you stretches the long, inviting runway. The air is crisp, the world is still, and it's just you and the plane. As you gently pull back on the control yoke, the plane responds. It's a perfect moment of unity, a harmony between pilot, machine, and nature. You feel the wheels leave the ground, and just like that, you're flying. The ground falls away beneath you, and you're soaring up into the dawning sky. It's moments like these that capture the pure joy of flying.

Flying also brings with it a sense of freedom unlike any other. Up in the sky, you can go in any direction you choose. Want to follow that river to see where it leads? Go for it! Want to circle around that cloud just because it looks interesting? Why not! As a pilot, you have the liberty to explore the sky in ways you can't on the ground. This freedom, this ability to carve your own path, is one of the most exciting aspects of flying.

And let's not forget about the views! From the cockpit, you'll see landscapes unfold beneath you in a way you've never seen before. The patchwork of fields, the shimmering surface of lakes, the sprawling cities, and the winding roads, all seem to take on a new life when viewed from above. It's like having a front-row seat to a never-ending show of Earth's beauty.

The excitement of flying doesn't stop when you

land. No, indeed! After the flight, there's the satisfaction of a job well done, the fun of debriefing and sharing stories with fellow pilots, and the anticipation of the next flight. And let's not forget about the cool pilot's logbook where you record details of every flight. Filling in the logbook after a successful flight gives you a sense of accomplishment and makes you look forward to the next entry.

In essence, the joy and excitement of flying isn't just about the act of piloting an aircraft. It's about the journey, the discovery, the challenges overcome, and the shared experiences. It's about the freedom and perspective that only come from being high above the ground. It's about fulfilling a dream and doing something that not everyone gets to do.

In this grand adventure of aviation, every flight is a section, every challenge is a lesson, and every success is a milestone. And the best part? This journey doesn't have an end. As long as there's sky above, there will always be new routes to explore, new skills to learn, and new heights to reach. So, here's to the joy and excitement of flying, the thrill of the takeoff, the beauty of the sky, and the satisfaction of a smooth landing. Here's to the dreamers, the doers, and the flyers. Because the sky isn't just the limit; it's home.

Made in United States
Orlando, FL
16 December 2024

55810758R00061